Uncle Hubbard
and the
Burlap Sack

Uncle Hubbard

and the

Burlap Sack

MARY SMITH HARDY

iUniverse, Inc.

Bloomington

Uncle Hubbard and the Burlap Sack

iUniverse books may be ordered through booksellers or by contacting:

iUniverse
1663 Liberty Drive
Bloomington, IN 47403
www.iuniverse.com
1-800-Authors (1-800-288-4677)

ISBN: 978-1-4759-0179-5 (sc)
ISBN: 978-1-4759-0180-1 (ebk)

Printed in the United States of America

iUniverse rev. date: 03/29/2012

This book is dedicated to my daughters—Adrienne,

Mironda, Maanami—and my grandchildren.

Thanks to my parents for giving lasting guidance and encouragement that continues to surface when needed with eagerness. MSH

Anonymous

Anonymus

Hello, children!

Allow me to take you on an adventure to a sandy and hilly countryside with gravel roads that are narrow and endless.

We'll be going on an adventure to the place where I lived my young and early adult years. The place was a farm owned and managed by my grandfather and father at a time when you had only a mule to do the plowing.

Get ready.

Come travel down memory lane to Sullivan Hollow, where I grew up and had the best summers of my life.

Let me introduce you to my uncle Hubbard and his burlap sack. It has been a long time and my memory is sometimes vague, but as I can recall, a burlap sack is usually brown with tiny holes.

This journey is but a snapshot of all the many wonderful memories I have from my early years growing up in Magee, Mississippi, in a place named Sullivan Hollow.

Sullivan Hollow was a lush and lovely place of hills and trees and fields, where I was born and raised as a kid.

There was never a dull moment in Sullivan Hollow!

It was a wide green place of shining, sandy clay soil and rolling hills that gave us big crops of fresh fruits and crisp vegetables.

The busy, buzzing bees were abundant and helped to pollinate the crop.

Anonymous

Families and friends were close to one another.

The people were purposeful, with plenty to do.

The grown-ups were poised and always ready for what life brought each day.

And what life brought each day for me back then were friends and family.

Sullivan Hollow was especially aromatic during the summer months.

When the green gardens blossomed with the flowers of the fruit trees and ripening vegetables, the air was rich with their pollen and perfume.

Anonymous

Anonymous

The big orange and golden-yellow blossoms of the honeysuckle vines were the hummingbirds' favorite flower—and mine too!

Over and around and through many garden fences, the honeysuckle vines flourished and gave their fresh fragrance on the winds of the warm countryside.

Bumblebees busily buzzed between the brushes and bushes of bountiful blossoms and buds.

They zipped and zapped and zigzagged here and there and then everywhere!

In the gardens, the grown-ups planted big heads of lettuce and cabbage, ruby-red radishes, catches of carrots, and skinny strings of sweet peas and beans.

Anonymous

In the large fields next to the family home and playground, my friends and I could find watermelons, cantaloupes, corn, cucumbers, field peas, and tomatoes as big as baseballs!

I remember how my momma would make valuable use of all the vegetables we grew in the garden.

She made potato soup tastier by adding fresh sweet peas, green beans, and carrots while she stirred, stewed, and hummed.

This was how she made sure we got all the vegetables we needed to grow up as big and strong as the grown-ups.

But do you want to know something?

I really, really did not like anything green! Especially vegetables!

Anonymous

If it was green and Momma said it was good for me, then I did not want to eat it!

Well . . . I cannot really say that I hated *everything* green, because my most favorite green things to eat when I was growing up were green apples and plums.

I would pass by a tremendous apple tree daily on my way to feed the pigs or when I was coming home from the field for lunch.

I would eat the apples straight from the tree till my face was sticky with their sweet juice.

Sometimes I would wait until I got home and let Momma bake an apple in the oven until it was soft and the aroma filled the kitchen.

Baked green apples were the best lunch to have in the summer!

Momma fussed and mussed at me for not eating enough other foods.

"Baby, you're going to be malnourished. You know you're not eating enough to stay alive and grow up at all," she would say.

But here I am, all grown up. I survived!

Sullivan Hollow was best known for its sweet peaches, green sour apples, and purple muscadine grapes.

Although time has passed and I only get a chance to be around every once in a while, I can still remember the charming smell and sweet taste of those muscadines.

Anonymus

There were bunches of muscadine vines growing in the middle of the cotton field when I was little.

My siblings and I really had to whack and wrestle and work our way through the weeds and greening cotton stalks to get those big purple wild grapes.

And believe me, we were determined to get our faces and hands all sticky, smelly, and colored purple with those grapes.

June bugs added a pleasant, lazy buzz to the summer air as they zimmed and zoomed and zapped around with the bumblebees.

When I was finished with all my chores, I would occasionally catch a june bug, tie a string to its tail, and let the insect fly above me as I walked along the dirt road.

Sometimes I would sit under a shady tree and let the june bug fly about like a kite till it broke free and flew away.

The happiness I enjoyed from green apples, sweet muscadine grapes, bumblebees, and siblings got even better when Uncle Hubbard came for a visit.

When Uncle Hubbard came to visit us, it was always a cause for excitement and cheer.

He did not live far from our house.

I could see the house that belonged to my uncle Hubbard and my auntie from where we lived.

"Papa's House" was what his brothers and sisters called the house where my daddy, momma, and siblings lived.

Anonymas

They called it that because they had grown up there as children too.

It was just down the narrow, curving road from my uncle Hubbard and auntie.

Uncle Hubbard's house was near the main country road, where the traffic of travelers that we saw flowed through the woods and down the gravel lane to the countryside.

Uncle Hubbard was my daddy's big brother. My cousins labeled him as my most favorite uncle.

When I told him so, he laughed and called me his "most favorite niece"! Sweet!

I could see him sitting on his porch sometimes, even from the window of our house.

Anonymous

He could tell you who passed by, at what time, and what kind of car they were driving.

My auntie, Uncle Hubbard's wife, was just as curious and just as observant as he was.

I remember my uncle Hubbard as a quiet yet jolly fellow who made us laugh.

He would visit us often in the morning or the evening.

When my dad married my mom, she came to Sullivan Hollow to live in his dad's house.

Momma always made Uncle Hubbard feel welcome when he visited while she was making breakfast in the morning or when she was making supper in the evening.

Anonymous

Anonymous

He never missed a day coming to visit our home, and he would stand near the screened door in the kitchen if the visit was during breakfast. He would watch my mother prepare breakfast, and sometimes he would drink a cup of coffee.

Because my daddy was the baby of the family, Uncle Hubbard wanted to make sure that all was well and that Daddy had everything he needed to take care of his family.

One of my favorite times with Uncle Hubbard was during the watermelon harvest one year.

Watermelon harvest took place during the late summer, just before it was time to go back to school.

Uncle Hubbard came to pay us a visit, as he always did.

Anonymous

On this particular hot summer evening, he shared stories about his day and his snuff, a powdered brown substance.

He knew Momma did not approve of him dipping snuff, which he placed in his bottom lip. It made his lip protrude from the bottom of his mouth.

He would give it to us, saying, "Ooh, it is sweet," with a mischievous twinkle in his eyes and a smile.

It was not sweet at all! It made us sick, and we would run to wash the taste out of our mouths with water or lemonade while Uncle Hubbard guffawed with laughter.

"Tsk, tsk, tsk. I told you so," Momma would scold us as she poured our drinks.

Anonymous

Anonymus

During watermelon harvest, Uncle Hubbard usually took a melon home to his wife and children, my auntie and cousins.

However, during one particular harvest, his mule, who was called Ole Joe, gave my uncle Hubbard the slip.

The melons and grain sacks were loaded on the mule's back when I found him eating in the cabbage patch later that day.

When I heard Uncle Hubbard's voice calling for Ole Joe, I stopped feeding the mule his cabbage and stuffed myself into one of the half-empty burlap sacks.

I wanted to surprise my auntie and cousins with a visit since I had not seen them during the day.

By the time Uncle Hubbard caught Ole Joe, the sun was setting and the crickets were singing.

I snickered a few times, holding my hands over my mouth. But I think my uncle Hubbard already knew I was in the sack. So he played along with me.

So up the road with Ole Joe and sacks of melons, vegetables, and a stowaway, Uncle Hubbard slowly made his way from the fields to his house, singing and whistling to himself all the way.

It was a short trip down the narrow, dusty road, so it wasn't long before we stopped.

Uncle Hubbard tied up Ole Joe for the night and started taking off the sacks.

Anonymus

The first bag he picked up to take into the house was mine.

When he entered his house, my auntie and little cousins gathered around him to take the watermelons and vegetables out of the sack.

They were surprised when suddenly I popped out of the sack instead of the watermelon!

My cousins laughed at the surprise. Uncle Hubbard made a big show of being shocked and wondering how his grain had turned into me all of sudden!

I smiled, saying hi to everybody, even though I must have looked a real mess standing there covered with grain and hay straw.

Anonymous

Uncle Hubbard winked at my auntie, and she shook her head and smiled.

I played with my cousins a long while, enjoying the sweetbread and milk that Auntie gave us.

It was a great surprise visit! But soon there came a knock at the door, and in came my daddy to take me back home.

He talked with Uncle Hubbard and Auntie for a while, but soon he scooped me up off the floor and we were both waving goodnight to everyone.

While he carried me on his shoulders back home to Momma and my brothers and sisters, I told him all about my day and how I had snuck into Uncle Hubbard's burlap sack.

Anonymous

Anonymus

It was a very good day!

———✦———

Many years later, after I had my own children and grandchildren, I often looked back and wondered about those times in Sullivan Hollow. I asked my mother about that late summer evening. She told me that after I had jumped into Ole Joe's feeding sack to hide, when Uncle Hubbard had passed by my mom and dad that evening, he had let them know I was there in the sack, safe and sound.

So you see, children, all was well right from the beginning.

And it was still a very good day.

Anonymous

The End

Printed in the United States
By Bookmasters